Original Title: 101 STRANGE BUT TRUE CATS FACTS

©101 STRANGE BUT TRUE CATS FACTS, Carlos Martínez Cerdá and Victor Martínez Cerdá, 2023

Authors: Victor Martínez Cerdá and Carlos Martínez Cerdá (V&C Brothers)

© Cover and illustrations: V&C Brothers

Layout and design: V&C Brothers

101

STRANGE BUT TRUE

CATS FACTS

INCREDIBLE AND SURPRISING FACTS

1

Cats are popular domestic animals worldwide.

Cats first appeared on Earth around 10.8 million years ago and are considered one of the oldest domesticated animals.

The ancestors of modern cats are believed to have evolved in Asia and spread to Europe and Africa.

Unlike dogs, cats were domesticated later in human history.

The first domesticated cats appeared about 4,000 years ago in ancient Egypt, where cats were worshipped and considered sacred.

Cats became popular animals in Egyptian households, where they were used to control pests like mice and other unwanted animals.

Egyptians adored cats so much that some even mummified them after death.

The abduction or sale of these animals could be punishable by death.

In addition, if a family cat died, all members of the family would shave their eyebrows as a sign of mourning.

The Egyptian word for cat is "mau."

The adoration of cats spread throughout the world, and today cats are one of the most popular pets.

Cats are independent, curious, and playful animals and can be trained to do tricks and to live indoors or outdoors.

2

Adult cats only meow to communicate with humans.

It is worth noting that they can make about 100 sounds, while dogs can only make 10.

Moreover, a cat has the ability to change its meow to get what it wants, even mimicking a baby's cry to get food.

They hiss to protect themselves and show that they are dangerous, the same way some snakes do.

Deaf cats make louder sounds than non-deaf ones.

There are breeds like the Siamese cat that are more talkative than others.

Most of the time, cats purr when they are happy, but females also do it when they are in labor, and sick or even scared cats to calm themselves.

In domestic cats, purring has a frequency between 25 and 150 vibrations per second.

3

Female cats are usually right-handed
and male cats are left-handed.

Those with a coat of three colors
are usually female.

It is very rare to find a male tricolor cat,
in fact, this alteration is due to
a chromosomal anomaly.

Therefore, 1 out of every 4,000 tricolor
cats is male and usually sterile.

Only 1 out of every 10,000 tricolor cats is a
fertile male. Not all cats have pink paw pads.

If it's black, they'll have black paw pads, if it's
light-colored, they'll have pink ones,
and if they have multiple colors,
they'll be multicolored.

4

Did you know that a cat's sense of smell is 14 times better than ours?

If their food has been in the bowl for a while, they may reject it because it smells bad.

A cat's nasal passages have 19 million nerve endings, while humans only have 5 million.

Cats don't have as developed a sense of smell as dogs, so their ability to detect odors serves other functions.

Cats use their sense of smell and scents to send or conceal information from other animals and not so much for hunting.

Cats dislike smells such as onion, vinegar, garlic, tobacco smoke, pepper, deodorants, eucalyptus, or citrus.

5

Cat whiskers act as sensors, helping them walk in the dark, calculate the space of a hole they want to squeeze through, and even hunt.

They are also indicators of their mood. Never cut your cat's whiskers.

They fall out every so often, but then grow back.

Both whiskers and hair are connected to their nervous system and respond to the slightest vibration.

6

Cats and other felines cannot detect sweet taste due to a genetic mutation.

Sugar detectors in the taste buds of felids are absent or do not function properly, preventing them from detecting sweet tastes.

This is because in the wild, felids do not need a sense of taste for sweet flavors, as their diet is primarily meat, which is rich in protein and fat.

Sweet flavors are not essential to their survival and therefore have not developed in their evolution.

Despite this, many cats show a preference for sweet-tasting foods, but this is more due to the texture and high fat content of the food than its sweet taste.

Butter and other high-fat foods are particularly attractive to cats because of their high caloric content, which provides them with a concentrated source of energy.

It is important to note that although cats cannot detect sweet tastes, they still have food preferences and can be very picky about their food.

In addition, cats have a very keen sense of smell, which can influence their food choice.

Therefore, it is important to provide cats with a balanced and high-quality diet to meet their nutritional needs and maintain their health.

7

The brain of a cat is similar in structure and function to the human brain.

In fact, it is estimated that cats have approximately 90% of the same brain structure as humans.

Both have a highly developed cerebral cortex, which is responsible for advanced cognitive functions such as sensory perception, memory, thinking, and learning.

Cats also have a very high capacity for learning and can learn to perform various tasks and tricks.

Compared to dogs, cats have better long-term memory, especially when it comes to learning something by doing it.

This is partly due to their ability to retain visual and spatial information, which allows them to remember how to perform complex tasks.

In addition, cats have a unique ability to adapt to new and unfamiliar situations, which allows them to survive and thrive in changing environments.

They are also very cunning and can solve problems with creativity and skill.

8

Over the years, cats can become lactose intolerant.

Lactose is a type of sugar present in milk
and dairy products.

Like other mammals, kittens produce an enzyme called
lactase, which helps them digest the lactose
in their mother's milk.

However, as kittens grow up and stop consuming
mother's milk, the production of lactase in their
digestive system gradually decreases.

This means that adult cats may have difficulty digesting
lactose and may experience symptoms such as diarrhea,
vomiting, and abdominal discomfort if they consume
too much milk or dairy products.

It is important to note that lactose intolerance is common
in many adult animals, including humans,
and is not exclusive to cats.

Additionally, not all cats experience lactose intolerance
and some may tolerate limited amounts of dairy
products without issue.

9

Cats are true athletes and are capable of jumping very high and with great precision thanks to a series of physical and mental skills.

One of the main reasons why cats are such good jumpers is due to the power of their hind legs.

The muscles in a cat's hind legs are very strong and allow them to push themselves upward with great force and speed.

Another reason why cats are such good jumpers is due to the flexibility of their spine.

Unlike humans, whose spine is rigid, a cat's spine is very flexible and allows them to twist and turn their body in amazing ways.

This enables them to perform complicated movements in the air while jumping.

Finally, cats' spatial awareness also plays a significant role in their jumping ability.

Cats have excellent depth and distance perception, which allows them to accurately calculate the trajectory of their jump and land precisely on their target.

10

Cats have 36 muscles in each ear and they function as parabolic antennas, directing them towards the source of sound.

They can rotate their ears 180 degrees and separately.

In addition, each ear has 32 muscles, which allow them to move towards each and every sound they perceive.

Felines are able to know where their prey is without even seeing or knowing where it is.

A blind cat can hunt thanks to its fine hearing.

11

When a cat rubs its body or head
against someone or something,
it is marking its territory.

They obey women better because they
perceive high-pitched sounds better.

However, the hearing ability
of cats is amazing.

They can hear sounds at 64 kHz.

We can only hear sounds up to 20 kHz.

12

Cats like to scratch vertical objects for several reasons.

First, scratching is an instinctive activity for cats that helps them keep their claws sharp and in good condition.

In nature, cats need to have sharp claws to hunt and defend themselves, so scratching is a natural way to keep their claws in good shape.

In addition, scratching can also be a way to exercise the muscles of the legs and the body in general.

When scratching, cats stretch and tense the muscles of their legs, shoulders, and back, which can be beneficial for keeping them strong and healthy.

Finally, it has been observed that many cats find scratching vertical objects, such as posts or scratching pads, to be relaxing and comforting.

When scratching, cats release built-up tension and can feel more calm and peaceful.

Additionally, scratching can be a way to mark territory and communicate with other cats through the pheromones they leave on the object.

It is important to note that if cats scratch inappropriate objects, such as furniture or curtains, it can be a problem for owners.

That's why it is recommended to provide them with an appropriate scratching post so that they can satisfy their need to scratch safely and without damaging other objects in the home.

13

Stubbs, a stray cat, became the honorary mayor of the small town of Talkeetna, Alaska, in 1997.

The town did not have an official mayor at the time, and residents were dissatisfied with all the candidates who ran for office, so someone suggested the idea of electing a cat as mayor.

Stubbs was elected honorary mayor by an overwhelming majority and became a popular tourist attraction in the town.

Despite having no real political powers, Stubbs served as the honorary mayor of Talkeetna for 15 years until his death in 2017.

As for the candidacy of a cat for the mayoralty of Mexico City in 2013, this was part of a publicity campaign to raise awareness about the importance of caring for and protecting stray animals.

A group of animal rights advocates presented a cat as a symbolic candidate for the mayoralty of Mexico City, but the candidacy had no real chance of winning since Mexican laws prohibit animals from running for political office.

The campaign was successful in drawing attention to the problem of stray animals in the city and the need to address this issue more effectively.

14

There is a popular belief in many parts of the world that black cats bring bad luck.

This superstition has existed since ancient times and has spread across many cultures.

For example, in medieval Europe, black cats were believed to be the companions of witches and could bring misfortune to a household.

In Italy and Spain, even today, it is believed that if a black cat crosses your path, it is a bad omen.

However, in other countries, such as Australia and the United Kingdom, the popular belief is quite the opposite.

Black cats are considered to be symbols of good luck.

In Scotland, for example, a black cat on the porch is believed to bring wealth and prosperity to the household.

In Japan, the black cat is seen as a protector and a symbol of good fortune.

It is important to note that these popular beliefs have no scientific basis, and black cats are no different than any other cat in terms of personality and behavior.

It is important to treat all cats with respect and love, regardless of their color.

15

Cats, like snakes and some other animals, have the Jacobson's organ, also known as the vomeronasal organ.

This organ is a sensory receptor located in the nasal cavity of many animals, including cats, and allows them to detect pheromones and other specific odors.

When a cat opens its mouth and wrinkles its upper lip, it is doing what is known as "flehmen".

This allows the air with the olfactory particles to come into contact with the Jacobson's organ, allowing them to more accurately analyze the odor in question.

Flehmen is a form of communication and natural behavior in many animals, and may be especially important for cats in terms of social communication and reproduction.

In addition, it is possible that cats also use this behavior to evaluate the safety of their environment and detect potential prey or nearby predators.

16

When a cat lies on its back, it is a sign that it feels safe and confident in its environment.

This is because exposing their belly is a vulnerable posture for cats, and they only do it when they feel safe and relaxed.

However, this does not necessarily mean that they want their belly rubbed, as some cats may react negatively to this.

Cats are known for being sleepy animals, and it is true that they spend most of the day sleeping.

On average, cats sleep between 16 and 18 hours a day, although some cats may sleep even more than that.

This is because cats are hunting animals and need a lot of energy to chase and capture prey, so their bodies adapt to conserve energy during moments of inactivity.

It is also true that many cats like to sleep with their back supported by something, like a wall or furniture.

This is because cats are territorial animals and need to always be alert to any possible threat.

By sleeping with their back supported, they can feel more secure that no one will approach them from behind without their notice.

17

Cats have a very wide peripheral vision that allows them to see almost 180 degrees, but their direct vision is more limited, as their central visual field is narrow.

This means that if something is right under their nose, their field of vision does not fully encompass it, which can lead them to not notice objects or food that are very close to their nose.

As for the unique nose, cats have a highly developed sense of smell that allows them to detect odors imperceptible to humans.

Each cat has a unique body odor that allows them to recognize each other, and they can also distinguish different odors in the environment.

Additionally, the cat's nose has a series of folds and crests that form a unique pattern in each individual, making it a sort of "fingerprint" that can be used for identification in some cases.

18

The oldest cat recorded in the Guinness Book of World Records was Creme Puff, who lived in Texas and died in 2005 at the age of 38 years and 3 days, making it the longest-lived domestic cat recorded in history.

However, it is important to note that most cats do not live that long, and the average lifespan of a domestic cat is around 12-16 years.

19

Most cats do not like to get wet or be in contact with water, although there are some exceptions.

This is partly because their fur is not as waterproof as that of other animals, which makes them uncomfortable when wet.

Additionally, cats are animals that do not need to be bathed, as they constantly groom themselves by licking their fur with their rough tongue, removing excess dirt and grease from their body.

However, it is important to note that not all cats hate water, and some even enjoy it.

Breeds like the Turkish Van cat or the Bengal cat have a natural love for water and may even play in it.

In general, it is important not to force a cat to be in contact with water if they are not comfortable, as this can cause them stress and anxiety.

20

Cats have a rough tongue that is covered in small protrusions called conical papillae, which are like tiny spikes that point backwards.

These papillae help cats groom their fur, catch and tear apart their prey's flesh, and lick up any liquid they want to drink.

The saliva they produce while grooming also serves an important function in removing dead hair and regulating their body temperature.

As for their taste capability, cats have around 473 taste receptors compared to humans who have around 9000, which means they don't have a wide variety of tastes like we do.

However, they have a natural preference for meat-flavored foods due to their carnivorous nature.

21

Cats have a natural instinct to bury their excrement in sand or soil, which is known as burying.

This behavior is due to their survival and defense instinct, as in nature strong odors can attract predators and signal their presence in the territory.

Additionally, cats are very clean animals and do not like to have their excrement near their resting or eating area.

By burying their excrement, they also avoid attracting insects and other scavenging animals.

22

Both Julius Caesar and Napoleon Bonaparte were known to have a fear of cats.

It is said that Julius Caesar believed that cats were magical beings and could see things that humans couldn't see.

During a battle in Egypt, Caesar reportedly ordered his soldiers not to harm any cats that crossed their path.

On the other hand, it is said that Napoleon Bonaparte had a phobia of cats due to a bad experience he had with one during his childhood.

According to legend, when he was a child, a cat jumped on him while he was in bed, which scared him and made him feel vulnerable.

Since then, Napoleon is said to have avoided the company of cats.

23

The cat Blackie is known as the world's richest cat, because his owner, a British millionaire named Ben Rea, left him an inheritance of 15 million pounds in her will.

Blackie was the last of the 15 cats that Rea had in her lifetime, and she decided to leave him all her fortune, making him one of the richest animals in the world.

After Rea's death in 1988, Blackie inherited her house and all her possessions.

Since then, the cat has been under the care of the lawyers who administer his inheritance and has appeared in various media outlets for his curious story.

24

The record for the largest non-fatal fall of a cat is very difficult to determine, as most of these incidents are not recorded.

However, there are some cases where cats have survived falls from very high heights.

One of the most famous cases is that of a cat named Andy, who in 1987 fell from the 16th floor of an apartment building in Boston, United States.

Despite the height, Andy survived the fall and only suffered a lung contusion and some scrapes.

It is believed that the fall may have been cushioned by the vegetation surrounding the building.

Although cats are known for their ability to land on their feet, this does not mean that they always survive falls from very high heights.

In fact, falls from more than two stories can be very dangerous for cats and can cause serious injuries or even death.

25

They have 3 eyelids.

The third eyelid of cats, also called the nictitating membrane, is hidden and is a semi-transparent, pink-colored membrane that is normally not visible but plays an important role in protecting the cat's eyes from dirt, foreign bodies, and microorganisms.

Why is it a good sign that it is not visible?

Because the normal position of the nictitating membrane is between the eye and the eyelids.

When the third eyelid remains visible, it is almost always a sign that the cat has a health problem.

26

Cats are territorial animals and often consider their home and nearby surroundings as their property.

When interacting with other cats or people, they typically use various signals to mark their territory and establish their hierarchical position.

One way that cats mark their territory is through rubbing, by rubbing their head and body against objects or people they consider important.

This action releases pheromones that indicate the presence of the cat in that place and identify it as part of the territory.

When a cat licks your hands, face, or hair, it may be demonstrating affection and acceptance towards you, but it may also be marking you with its scent so that other cats or animals know that you are part of its group.

Additionally, some experts suggest that cats may also lick people to show submission or to request attention and care.

In any case, the cat's behavior is typically motivated by its need to mark its territory and establish social relationships with other living beings.

Nepeta cataria, also known as catnip or catmint, is a plant that belongs to the mint family and produces an effect of excitement and euphoria in most cats, although not all.

The chemical compound responsible for this effect is nepetalactone, which is found in the leaves and stems of the plant.

When cats come into contact with Nepeta cataria, they may exhibit strange behaviors such as rubbing, rolling, licking, and chewing on the plant, and some may even meow or purr.

Although the plant is not addictive or toxic to cats, some pet owners may find their cats' behavior after consuming it to be annoying or even destructive, so its use is recommended to be limited.

It should be noted that not all cats react to Nepeta cataria, and its effect may last for a few minutes or up to an hour, depending on the cat and the amount of plant ingested.

Cats see in color.

For a long time, it was believed that cats had monochromatic vision, meaning that they couldn't distinguish colors.

However, recent studies have shown that this is not the case and that, on the contrary, cats are capable of seeing different colors, albeit in a limited way.

At night, they can only see in black and white.

The eyes of cats have a layer of cells behind the retina called the tapetum lucidum, which helps the cat to double the little light it receives when it is dark.

During the day and when there is more light, they can distinguish between red and blue, although they don't seem to differentiate between green, yellow, and white.

It is thought that they perceive red as a dark gray.

A cat's tail can be an important indicator of its mood and communication.

Some examples of what a cat's tail can indicate include:

▪ If the tail is raised in a vertical position with the tip slightly curved to one side, it's a sign that the cat is happy and friendly.

▪ If the tail is bristled and appears larger than normal, it's a sign that the cat is scared or aggressive.

▪ If the tail is low and moving slowly, it may indicate that the cat is insecure or unsure of what's happening around it.

▪ If the tail is moving rapidly from side to side, it's a sign that the cat is angry or frustrated.

Of course, these are just some of the signals that a cat's tail can send, and each cat is different.

It's important to pay attention to other indicators of behavior, such as the cat's overall body language, to understand its mood.

30

Isaac Newton, one of the most important scientists in history, in addition to his contributions to physics and mathematics, was also a cat lover.

It is said that he had several felines that he cared for with care and dedication, so much so that he built a special door for one of them so it could come and go from his house at will, without anyone having to open it.

This cat door, known as a "cat flap" in some places, has become popular over time and remains a very useful tool for cat owners who want to give them the freedom to enter and exit the house without having to open and close the door every time they wish.

31

How do cats sweat?

Cats do produce sweat, although in smaller
amounts than humans as they have
fewer sweat glands.

Their sweat glands are located between
the paw pads, chin, anus, and lips.

On hot and humid days, your feline may leave
sweat marks on the floor of your house.

It is worth noting that cats do not sweat to
regulate their body temperature like humans do.

Instead, they use other mechanisms to stay cool,
such as licking their fur to wet it and then letting
air circulate through it and evaporate,
which helps to cool their body.

They can also pant and breathe faster to
eliminate heat from their body.

However, in situations of stress or fear,
cats may sweat more than usual.

32

Signs that your cat is scared:

- Escaping or hiding more than usual: cats like to have safe places to retreat to, but if you notice your furry friend hiding more than usual, it may be because they are afraid. It's important to let your cat stay in their safe space and let them come out at their own pace. If they stay there for a while, make sure their food and water dishes are accessible. They may come out for a quick bite and then retreat back to their hiding spot until they feel it's safe to come out again.

- Changes in bathroom habits: if your cat is scared, they may want to urinate or defecate inside, so make sure they have access to their litter box, but remember not to place it too close to their food.

- Over-grooming: if you notice your cat grooming excessively, it could be a sign of anxiety. Excessive grooming can cause hair loss, bald spots, or even damage to the skin and already damaged areas.

- Less interaction: this may be because they are aware of distant noises that scare them. They may just need some quiet time in their favorite hiding spot.

- Body language: arched back, flat ears, and backward-pointing whiskers are some signs that your cat is scared and anxious.

33

What can I do to make my cat more comfortable traveling?

Cats love the familiar.

You know your cat's favorite spot at home, so why not leave their carrier there for a few days before traveling?

To make it even more enticing, why not put their favorite blanket and toys inside?

Your cat will begin to see the carrier as a familiar and pleasant place.

Cats can get motion sickness, but it can be prevented by leaving 6 hours between their last meal and the scheduled departure time.

Make sure to keep them hydrated on long trips, especially when it's hot.

In case of any "accidents," put something absorbent at the bottom of the carrier.

Remember that the carrier is there to protect them and should be secured with a seat belt when you're driving and ideally in the least vibrating area of the car.

To help your cat stay calm, you can also place a towel or blanket over the carrier so they see fewer unfamiliar things.

34

Slow blinking is a nonverbal communication signal that cats use to express calmness, relaxation, and confidence.

When a cat blinks slowly, it closes its eyes partially or completely for more than half a second and then opens them slowly.

This behavior is considered a sign that the cat feels comfortable and secure in its environment and with the person or animal in front of it.

In a recent study from the United Kingdom published in the journal Scientific Reports, researchers analyzed cats' response to human slow blinking.

They found that when a human blinks slowly at a cat, the cat tends to respond with a slow blink back, indicating that cats are capable of recognizing the behavior and responding to it.

This finding suggests that humans can use slow blinking as a way to communicate with cats and establish a positive connection with them.

35

Foods that cats cannot eat:

–Raw eggs: They don't sit well with them, so they can only eat cooked eggs in very small pieces and quantities.

–Cereals: Bread, cereal... can make it difficult for your cat to digest and cause discomfort, so it's best to avoid them. Monitor the composition of the cat food to ensure that the amount of cereal it contains is appropriate.

–Some plants are toxic to them: poinsettia, oleander, and lily of the valley.

–Industrial sweets and sugar: especially those present in cookies, cakes, and industrial sweets... are very harmful to cats.

–Oranges and grapes: grapes and raisins can cause kidney problems in cats, and on the other hand, citrus fruits will cause discomfort and stomach upset.

–Chocolate, coffee, and tea: all three are completely prohibited in the cat's diet, as they can even cause death.

–Some vegetables: onion, garlic, potato, and tomato.

–Alcohol and aspirin: cats do not digest alcohol well and can become intoxicated, which can be lethal in some cases.

How does cat allergy develop?

Cat allergy is a very common public health problem in human medicine.

This allergy is mediated by immunoglobulin E (IgE) and generally presents with ocular problems (red and watery eyes) and nasal problems (secretions, itching in the nose...).

Cats develop several antigens that can cause these allergies in people, being in most cases caused by the Fel d1 protein.

In fact, studies carried out on people allergic to cats show that 90% of them have IgE against this protein.

This protein, Fel d1, is excreted in salivary and sebaceous glands, presenting a high concentration in saliva.

When a cat grooms itself, it spreads this protein all over its body and skin, and it comes off along with hair and dander.

This protein is small in size and very volatile, so it can remain in the environment and on surfaces such as clothing, sofas, and carpets.

37

Feromones are chemical substances that animals emit to communicate with other individuals of their species.

They are detected by a specialized organ called the vomeronasal organ (VNO), which is located in the nasal cavity.

Cats have a highly developed VNO, which allows them to detect pheromones with great precision.

In the case of cats, pheromones play a very important role in their sexual and social behavior.

Males can detect the smell of pheromones from females in heat through their sense of smell, which allows them to identify sexually receptive females and, therefore, have a chance to mate.

Additionally, cats can also detect the pheromones of other cats to obtain information about their mood, stress level, and territory.

For example, cats can leave urine marks containing pheromones to mark their territory and communicate with other cats.

In scientific research, various techniques have been developed to detect pheromones in animals.

Some of these techniques include chemical analysis of substances in urine and saliva, as well as the use of devices that measure animals' physiological responses to pheromones.

38

The vast majority of newborn kittens have blue eyes.

However, this is not due to their natural eye color, but rather a translucent layer that covers the iris.

This layer gradually disappears in the first few weeks of life, allowing the true color of the iris to become visible.

The final eye color of a cat is determined by its genetics and can range from green, yellow, amber, orange, and brown.

The development of a cat's definitive eye color varies by breed and individual, but generally occurs around 6 to 12 weeks of age.

It is possible for a cat to have eyes of different colors, which is known as heterochromia.

This is also determined by genetics and can be a hereditary trait or acquired due to injury or illness.

As for the sexual and physical maturity of cats, they generally reach sexual maturity at 5-6 months of age.

At this point, cats can begin to reproduce and exhibit typical adult behaviors.

However, full physical maturity is not reached until around 2 years of age, at which point cats reach their adult size and weight.

Cats also experience changes as they age. The senior years in cats begin around 10 years of age.

As cats age, they may experience changes in their health, such as mobility issues, kidney disease, and dental problems.

It is important that older cats receive regular veterinary care and specialized care to ensure their well-being and quality of life in their later years.

39

**Americans spend a significant amount of money
on cat food every year.**

In fact, according to some studies, pet food expenses
in general exceed expenses on baby food.

According to the American Pet Products Association, it is estimated
that Americans spent around $30.32 billion on pet food in 2020.

Of this amount, approximately $10.95 billion was spent on cat food.

On the other hand, it is estimated that Americans spend
around $7 billion on baby food each year.

There are several reasons for this, one of which is the fact that cats
are one of the most popular pets in the United States.

Many cat owners consider their pets as part of the family and are
willing to spend a significant amount of money on their food and care.

In addition, the pet food industry has evolved to offer
a wide variety of options for pet owners.

There are cat foods available in different flavors, formulations,
and prices to meet the needs and preferences of cat owners.

Although the expense on pet food may be high, it is important to
remember that expenses on baby food include a wide variety of
products, such as infant formulas, cereals, fruits and vegetables, and
organic baby food. Parents may also spend a significant amount of
money on diapers and other essential baby products.

In any case, both pet food and baby food are important expenses for
American families and it is important to ensure that these expenses
are appropriate for each family's budget and needs.

40

White cats with blue eyes may have unique health problems compared to other cats.

White cats with blue eyes are a special type of cat that have a genetic mutation that causes a lack of pigmentation.

This lack of pigmentation is known as partial albinism.

As a result, white cats with blue eyes have a bright white coat and light blue eyes.

However, the lack of pigmentation in their skin and eyes can make them more prone to certain health problems.

In particular, many white cats with blue eyes are born deaf or have hearing problems due to how the lack of pigmentation affects their inner ears.

Additionally, due to the lack of pigmentation, the skin of white cats with blue eyes is very sensitive to sunlight.

They are prone to sunburns and developing skin cancer if not properly protected from the sun.

Therefore, it's important for owners of white cats with blue eyes to keep them indoors or protect them from the sun with clothing or sunscreen for cats.

41

Cats are one of the most popular pets worldwide, with over 500 million domestic cats of more than 40 breeds.

Cats are animals that have been domesticated by humans for thousands of years, and are believed to have been selectively bred to create different breeds with specific characteristics.

Among the most popular cat breeds are Siamese, Persian, Sphynx, Maine Coon, and Bengal, among others.

Each breed has its own personality and distinctive physical characteristics such as size, coat, and head shape.

Domestic cats are very popular as pets due to their independent and affectionate personalities, as well as their ability to provide companionship and entertainment to their owners.

They are also very clean and require little maintenance compared to other pets, making them a popular choice for those with busy schedules or living in apartments.

Additionally, cats are very versatile animals and have been used for various purposes throughout history.

For example, they have been used as pest hunters on farms and ships to keep rodents at bay.

They have also been used as therapy animals and to assist people with disabilities, such as cats trained to alert their owners to dangerous sounds or situations.

They can fit into impossible spaces.

Their skeleton and musculature not only allows them to be agile climbers or hunters, but also to fit into practically any space, no matter how small it may seem.

How many times have you seen your cat squeeze into a tiny box or crawl into a space smaller than its body?

Now, why do they do this?

The answer is simple: it produces a sense of security, protection, and/or warmth for them.

Depending on the type of hiding place they decide to access, the reasons may vary, but the fact of squeezing into a smaller space produces a greater sense of protection for them.

43

Waffle is a famous cat known for his impressive jumping ability, which earned him the Guinness World Record for the longest jump by a cat.

He was born in Canada and was adopted by his owner, Julie Zielinski, when he was a kitten.

In 2018, Waffle became a Guinness World Record holder after jumping a distance of 213.36 centimeters (7 feet and 0.09 inches) from the ground to a platform.

This achievement made him the cat with the longest jump in the world.

Waffle is a Savannah cat, which is a hybrid breed resulting from the crossing of a domestic cat and an African serval.

This breed is known for being active, curious, and intelligent, which could explain his jumping ability.

In addition to his jumping ability, Waffle is known for his friendly personality and love for water.

He enjoys swimming in the pool at his home and playing with water sprays.

44

Towser was a tortoiseshell cat who lived at the Glenturret whisky distillery in Crieff, Scotland, for much of her life.

The distillery is known for producing Famous Grouse whisky, and Towser became a tourist attraction due to her mouse-catching abilities.

It is said that Towser began her hunting career as a kitten and quickly proved to be a formidable hunter.

It is reported that during her life, Towser caught and killed nearly 29,000 mice at the distillery, earning her the Guinness World Record for the cat with the most mice caught.

Towser died in 1987 at the age of 24, but her legacy lives on at the distillery.

In her honor, a statue has been erected and her story has been told in various books and documentaries.

In addition to her hunting abilities, Towser was said to be a friendly and affectionate cat who liked to be close to people and receive attention.

Her legacy has shown that cats can be useful in places like distilleries and farms, where they can keep rodent and other unwanted animal populations under control.

45

Colonel Meow was a Himalayan-Persian breed cat who became famous for his lush fur and grumpy facial expression.

He won the Guinness World Record in 2014 for having the longest fur of any domestic cat, with a length of 22.87 centimeters.

Colonel Meow was born in 2011 and was adopted by his owners, Anne Marie Avey and Eric Rosario, when he was a kitten.

He soon became famous on social media for his unique look and grumpy attitude.

In 2013, Colonel Meow was named the world's grumpiest cat by the BuzzFeed website.

His fame continued to grow, and in 2014, he won the Guinness World Record for the cat with the longest fur.

In addition to his distinctive appearance, Colonel Meow was also known for his friendly and playful personality.

He liked to play with toys and spend time with his owners.

Sadly, Colonel Meow passed away in January 2014 at the age of 2 due to complications from surgery.

However, his legacy continues, and his photos and videos remain popular on social media.

Different types of marking:

-Urinary marking: they usually spray urine in a sprinkler-like manner on vertical objects mainly to delimit their territory.

-Facial marking: they also have glands on their face that release pheromones, so through this marking, they leave a chemical (olfactory) signal that they or other cats can perceive. They rub their face against objects, animals or people to leave that signal. It is not a way of marking something as "theirs," but rather to indicate that that place, animal, or person is safe and trustworthy.

-Paw marking: their paws also contain glands that release pheromones, so this marking is done by scratching surfaces or objects.
Thus, they leave a chemical and visual signal. They can do this when they feel stressed or for reproductive purposes.

47

**Many people wonder why cats
knead so often.**

When they are babies, cats knead their
mother's nipples to stimulate
milk production.

It is a natural movement that not only
provides them with food but also
strengthens the bond and generates a
feeling of well-being, safety, and pleasure.

When they are adults, cats knead people
or objects to express that they are calm,
happy, and feel secure.

For this reason, your cat kneading you is a
clear sign that they love you, trust you,
and are happy by your side.

48

They are crepuscular animals.

By nature, cats are not diurnal animals, but concentrate their activity during twilight, that is, at dusk and dawn.

This is a survival mechanism adopted by the species to avoid their predators and to be able to hunt their prey, which also tend to be crepuscular.

When adopting a kitten, it is common to perceive that it is more active at night, which can frustrate us if we see that we cannot get them to sleep and let us sleep.

However, it is important to keep in mind that this is their nature and that modifying this aspect may take some time, so it is essential to have patience and resort to education techniques that do not disturb the animal's well-being.

49

They don't like stagnant water.

How many times have you seen your
cat drinking water from the tap
or with their paw?

The explanation is simple:
cats prefer moving water.

They are extremely neat and intelligent
animals, so they can detect if the water
has not been renewed and,
therefore, is dirty.

Similarly, fresh moving water, such as the
one they would drink from a river in the
wild, does not accumulate pathogens,
so they avoid certain diseases.

50

**Many cats seem to have a sagging belly,
even if they are not overweight.**

This is due to the presence of the so-called primordial
pouch, which is a fold of loose and flexible skin
in the belly area of cats.

The primordial pouch is a feature inherited by domestic
cats from their wild ancestors, who used it to store
fat during times of food scarcity and to protect
the abdominal area during fights and
movement on uneven terrain.

Although the primordial pouch is not necessary for the
survival of domestic cats, it is still a feature present in
many of them, especially those who have a genetic
predisposition to have more fat in the abdomen.

It is important to note that the presence of the primordial
pouch should not be confused with overweight or obesity.

It is possible for a cat to have a primordial pouch and,
at the same time, a healthy weight.

Therefore, if there are doubts about a cat's weight,
it is recommended to take them to the
vet for a full evaluation.

51

International Cat Day is a date dedicated to honoring and promoting the welfare of cats.

Although it was established in honor of "Socks", the Clinton family cat, its aim is to raise awareness among the world population about the importance of cats as pets and to encourage responsible adoption of homeless cats.

During this day, various activities are carried out around the world, such as adoption events, donations to animal shelters, sterilization and castration campaigns, among others.

In addition, on social media, photos and videos of cats are usually shared with the hashtag #InternationalCatDay.

It is important to note that International Cat Day also aims to raise awareness about the problems that cats face worldwide, such as abandonment, mistreatment, and lack of proper veterinary care.

It seeks to promote a culture of respect and care towards these animals, as well as to encourage their protection and conservation.

Cat urine can glow in the dark when illuminated with black light.

This is due to the presence of certain chemicals in the urine, such as urochrome, which can be fluorescent under certain conditions.

The fluorescence of cat urine can be useful in identifying if your cat is marking territory in the house, as urine stains can be difficult to detect with the naked eye, especially if they are small or in dark places.

By illuminating the area with black light, the urine marked by your cat will glow and be easier to detect.

However, it is important to note that the fluorescence of urine does not always indicate that the cat is marking territory.

Urine can also glow under certain natural conditions, such as when the cat has eaten foods rich in vitamin B or has been exposed to certain medications or chemicals.

In any case, if you suspect that your cat is marking territory in the house, it is important to take steps to prevent this from happening in the future.

This can include providing enough clean and accessible litter boxes, limiting the cat's access to certain areas of the house, or seeking help from a veterinarian or an animal behavior specialist if the problem persists.

53

In 1879, an experiment was conducted in the United Kingdom that used cats to deliver mail to some nearby towns.

The idea behind this project was that cats, being intelligent and agile animals, could transport mail more quickly than postal workers on foot.

The experiment involved tying a mailbag to each cat's neck and letting them go on their own to the destination.

However, the project quickly failed because the cats were not disciplined enough to follow a specific path or deliver the mailbag to the right place.

Instead, the cats often got distracted by other animals, chased birds, or simply went off their designated route.

In addition, some cats returned home instead of continuing with the task, making the mail delivery process even slower.

After several unsuccessful attempts, the project was abandoned and it was decided that postal workers on foot would remain the best option for mail delivery.

54

Cats are very clean animals and constantly devote themselves to personal grooming.

Cats have a rough and flexible tongue that allows them to effectively lick and groom their fur.

It is estimated that a cat can dedicate up to 30% of its waking time to grooming its fur.

Personal grooming is important for cats for several reasons.

Firstly, it helps them to keep their fur clean and free of dirt and food debris.

It also helps them regulate their body temperature, as when they lick themselves, cats moisten their fur with saliva, which allows them to cool down on hot days.

In addition, personal grooming can also have a calming effect on cats, helping them to relax and reduce stress.

However, it is important to note that cats can swallow a significant amount of hair during their grooming, which can lead to the formation of hairballs in their digestive tract.

These hairballs can cause digestive problems in cats, so it is important to regularly brush the cat's fur and provide them with an appropriate diet to prevent their formation.

55

During the first few weeks of life, it is essential that kittens learn to relate to humans and feel safe and comfortable in their presence.

In fact, experts recommend that kittens be handled and stroked by humans from a very young age so that they become accustomed to human presence and become social and affectionate cats.

In addition, once cats have established a bond with their humans, they are often very loyal and affectionate.

They can show affection in various ways, such as purring, rubbing against their owners' legs, curling up in their laps, or following them around the house.

It is important to note that each cat is unique and has its own personality, so some may be more independent than others, while others may be very needy of human attention and companionship.

However, in general, cats are very capable of creating bonds with humans and enjoy the company and affection of their owners.

56

Cats have unique personalities and can decide when they do or do not want to receive pets or attention.

Some cats like to be in contact with humans all the time, while others like to have their space and moments of solitude.

It is important to respect each cat's boundaries and not force contact if the cat does not want it.

However, if a cat bites or scratches during a petting session, it is not necessarily because they are tired.

It can be a sign that the cat is uncomfortable or overstimulated and needs a break.

Cats have a threshold of tolerance to tactile stimulation, and it is important to learn to read the signals of their body language to avoid exceeding that threshold and causing them stress or discomfort.

As for the idea that cats are owners and masters of your life, it is true that they can have attitudes of dominance and control in certain situations, but this does not mean that you cannot establish boundaries and rules for their behavior.

With proper and consistent training, cats can learn to behave respectfully and adapt to the routines and rules of the home.

57

A cat's tail is an important indicator of their mood and nonverbal communication.

If your cat has their tail up and moving gently from side to side, it is a sign that they are content and happy.

On the other hand, if the tail is stiff and raised straight up, it may indicate an aggressive or alert attitude.

If the tail is low and close to the body, it may be a sign of fear or submission.

Additionally, cats can also move the tip of their tail quickly and repeatedly when they are excited or irritated, and they may wrap it around themselves as a form of protection or comfort.

58

Many cats love to hide in closets and drawers, especially those that have soft clothes or fabrics inside.

This is because cats have a natural instinct to seek shelter and security in tight, protected places that give them a sense of being in a safe and controlled environment.

In addition, closets and drawers are often quiet and dark places where cats can rest undisturbed, and they also provide an opportunity for them to feel closer to their owners by being in a space that smells like them.

Therefore, if you have a cat at home, it is important to make sure that there is no potential danger inside the cabinets, such as chemicals or loose cables, and that your cat can easily get out if it wants to.

Cats have a natural instinct for conserving energy, and this includes food.

In nature, a cat doesn't know when it will catch its next prey, so it has to ration its food and be able to survive with few meals for several days.

This tendency has even persisted in domestic cats that are well-fed and don't have to worry about finding their food.

Domestic cats also have the ability to regulate their own food intake.

As long as they have constant access to food, cats can take small portions throughout the day instead of eating everything at once.

Additionally, if a cat feels full or satisfied, it will not continue eating, which means that cats are less prone to overeating compared to other animals.

However, it is important to note that some cats may have weight or health issues that affect their ability to regulate their food intake.

It is important to monitor the amount and quality of food we give our cats, and work with a veterinarian to ensure that they are healthy and at an appropriate weight.

Having a cat can have benefits for human health.

According to several studies, petting a cat and listening to their purring can lower blood pressure and reduce stress, which in turn can reduce the risk of cardiovascular diseases.

Additionally, having a cat can improve mood and reduce symptoms of anxiety and depression.

It has also been shown that older people who have a cat are less likely to suffer a hip fracture.

Another benefit of having a cat is that they can help reduce feelings of loneliness and provide companionship and affection to their owners.

Additionally, having a cat can foster responsibility and commitment, as they require daily care and attention.

However, it is important to note that having a cat also comes with responsibilities and associated costs, such as providing them with proper nutrition, veterinary care, and maintaining their hygiene and well-being.

61

What is the lifespan of a cat?

The lifespan of a domestic cat is about 15 years, but it's important to know that not all years are proportionally equivalent to human years, as cats age more slowly.

Although the data is not exact, you can get an idea of your cat's human age using these calculations:

-First year: equivalent to 15 human years.

-Second year: equivalent to 10 human years.

-Third-ninth year: each year is equivalent to 7 human years.

-From 10 years onwards: each year is equivalent to 4 human years.

Example: if your cat is 4 years old, it is equivalent to 39 human years (15+10+7+7).

62

They walk on their toes.

Cats don't walk by supporting their whole foot, but rather they do it like dancers, walking on the tips of their toes.

This condition increases the gracefulness and elegance of their movements and also helps them to hunt silently.

In addition, they walk and run by moving their front and back legs on the same side.

Only camels, giraffes, and cats have this particularity.

They have a common origin.

According to research published in the journal Science, their most recent ancestor was born over 100,000 years ago in the Near East and belonged to the African wild species Felis Silvestris Lybica.

After analyzing the genomes of 979 cats, it was observed that their genetic branches were related.

This means that both domestic cats and several wild species come from a lineage before those 100,000 years, when Homo Sapiens began to leave Africa towards Eurasia and shared land with Neanderthals.

64

They know their name, if they don't obey it's because they don't want to.

Cats recognize their name when someone talks to them, according to a study by a group of Japanese researchers led by Atsuko Saito from the University of Sophia, Tokyo.

Although these little felines apparently do not obey in the same way as dogs, it turns out that they do know when they are being called.

They recognize their name and differentiate it from other words with the same length and intonation, even if the person saying it is someone they don't know.

In summary, if your cat doesn't come when you want it to, it's because it doesn't feel like it, but it has understood you.

65

A cat's heart beats on average between 140 and 220 times per minute, which is significantly faster than the human heart, which beats on average between 60 and 100 times per minute.

This is because cats have a higher metabolism than humans, which means their body processes and burns energy more quickly.

Regarding coat color, there is no scientific evidence to support that black cats are calmer than white cats or vice versa.

A cat's behavior depends on individual factors such as their personality, life experience, health, and socialization, not their coat color.

It is important to remember that stereotypes about cat behavior based on coat color are not accurate and can lead to unfair prejudice and discrimination against certain cats.

66

The legend of a cat's seven lives is a popular belief that has existed for centuries in different cultures around the world.

According to this legend, cats have seven lives, which means they can survive dangerous situations or accidents that would have killed any other animal.

The history behind this belief is uncertain, although there are several theories about it.

One theory is that it comes from ancient Egyptian culture, which considered cats as sacred beings and attributed them with a lot of special powers and abilities.

It was believed that cats were able to enter and leave the world of the dead and had the ability to heal the sick.

Another theory is that the legend of a cat's seven lives originated in Europe during the Middle Ages, when cats were persecuted and considered devilish animals by the Catholic Church.

It was said that cats were able to escape death thanks to their agility and dexterity and could survive falls from great heights.

Although the idea of a cat having seven lives is just a legend and has no scientific basis, it is true that cats have a great ability to survive dangerous situations and escape from situations that could be deadly for other animals.

This is due to their agility, speed, and innate survival skills, which make them fascinating and mysterious animals.

67

Hunting instinct is an inherent characteristic in cats, and it is common to see them playing and hunting imaginary objects or prey from an early age.

However, to become really effective hunters, cats need to learn from their mother during the nursing period.

During this time, the mother cat teaches them how to stalk, chase, and capture prey.

Additionally, she also teaches them to distinguish between objects or animals that may be dangerous to them.

It is important to note that, although domestic cats do not need to hunt to survive, the hunting instinct is still present in them and they may hunt small animals such as rodents, insects, and birds, which can generate controversy among cat owners.

For this reason, it is important to keep domestic cats in a safe and controlled environment, and prevent them from going out to hunt in nature.

68

Cats lose a significant amount of fluid while cleaning themselves with their rough and scratchy tongue.

It is estimated that they can lose up to 25% of their body fluid while grooming.

This is especially relevant in warm and dry climates, where it is important for cats to drink enough water to stay hydrated and prevent dehydration.

Additionally, if the cat is sick or has any health problems, it may lose even more fluids than normal, which in turn could worsen the situation.

For this reason, it is important to ensure that cats have constant access to fresh and clean water, especially during the warmer months of the year.

The first cat, known as Proailurus, weighed around 20 pounds and spent most of its time hanging from trees.

It had a long, slender body resembling that of a modern-day civet, and compared to the modern cat, had more teeth and a less complex brain.

Then, after 10 million years of evolution, Pseudaelurus emerged.

While this species still had a longer body, it had teeth similar to those of today's cats.

From Pseudaelurus came two different relatives: the saber-toothed cats, which went extinct along with their prey about 10,000 years ago, and Felinae.

Domestication.

While ancient Egyptians were close to their domestic cats, widespread domestication as we know it today did not take place until the 18th century.

However, before humans brought cats into their homes, we already had an ongoing mutually beneficial relationship; they often lived near our settlements and helped keep them free of rodents.

After the ancient Egyptians, it would not be until around the 17th century in Europe that the status of the cat would begin to change from being a useful mouse hunter to a beloved pet.

Cats and witchcraft.

In centuries past, cats were sometimes viewed as magical beings, even tagged as sinister creatures that were linked to witchcraft.

Some of these ideas likely stem from the fact that cats behave differently from other domestic animals.

Unlike dogs, cats are independent and self-sufficient.

They certainly aren't eager to please.

These traits haven't always been appreciated.

From the Middle Ages to more modern times, some people saw cats' unwillingness to obey commands, their stealthy maneuvers, and their active nighttime lives as ungodly behavior.

Starting from the 16th century, these unique characteristics, along with the belief that cats could mysteriously disappear and reappear out of nowhere, made cats labeled as agents of witchcraft.

Anyone who had a cat would often be suspected of being a witch and would be judged, especially if they were friendly with their cats or were seen talking to them.

"The Trial of Lincoln's Cat".

It occurred in 1791 in the city of Plymouth, Massachusetts (USA).

A local family's baby died mysteriously, and a black stray cat was seen lurking around the house during the time of death.

Neighbors began to suspect that the cat was the cause of the death, and a local woman was accused of being a witch and of sending the cat to kill the baby.

The trial took place in the Lincoln court, where the cat was presented as evidence.

The feline was examined by veterinarians and declared to have a normal attitude and show no signs of being involved in the baby's death.

However, superstition and fear of black cats were common at the time, and the cat was eventually declared guilty and ordered to be executed.

Fortunately, the idea that a cat can "suck" a person's breath and kill them is simply a myth.

In reality, cats are clean and energetic animals that rarely present health problems that can affect humans.

Although cats can be dangerous to small pets such as birds and rodents, there is no evidence indicating that cats are dangerous to humans.

Witches who turn into cats.

Over time, cats were also seen as the creatures in which a shape-shifting witch could transform when she wanted to hide her identity.

This is what Elizabeth Morse was accused of and found guilty of in the 17th century; Morse supposedly transformed into a cat-like creature to attack her neighbor.

According to the story, the neighbor defended himself and left marks that were discovered on Morse's body the next day.

All of these superstitions resulted in cats often being horribly abused over the years.

In France, during the 17th and 18th centuries, cats accused of being demons were hung from May poles.

And Christian communities in this same period even burned cats alive in the hope that such rituals would lead to a bountiful harvest and drive away evil spirits.

Over time, people became less superstitious, and as you will learn, there are less sinister views on what cats represent.

The cat, a symbol of female sexuality.

Cats have been associated with femininity since ancient Egypt, where the goddess Bastet had feline features and represented motherhood and sexual appeal.

It's possible that this all started because cats are soft, pretty, and elegant, which are traditionally traits associated with attractive women.

And this hasn't changed; the image of a cat is still considered feminine, while the image of a dog is mainly considered masculine.

This representation can also be seen in many works of art: in Francesco Bacchiacca's portrait of a young woman with a cat, dating back to 1525, a young woman cradles a cat in her arms, whose open-eyed stare serves to represent the blossoming sexuality of the woman.

The cat and prostitution.

For centuries, cats have also symbolized prostitution.

Since the 1400s, prostitutes have been called "cats" because of the animal's natural sense of self-preservation.

Known for the time they spend grooming themselves, "cat" was seen as an appropriate name for prostitutes who beautified themselves to make a living.

The naturalist and writer Alphonse Toussenel made direct and rather unfavorable comparisons between cats and prostitutes in his 1855 book Zoologie Passionelle.

Here, he referred to both as animals that take care of themselves, enjoy loud orgies, and are unsuitable for long-term relationships.

76

Marine Sergeant Frank Praytor feeds a newly adopted orphaned kitten during the Korean War in 1952.

The story began when one of his comrades cruelly shot a cat that wouldn't stop meowing.

Under the dead animal, they found two newly born kittens.

Praytor decided to adopt one of them and named her Miss Hap.

Another soldier did the same for her sister, but she didn't survive.

Praytor fed Miss Hap with milk mixed with water, then with canned meat, and the kitten managed to pull through.

When Praytor had to return to his country, he left Miss Hap in an information office, safe and in charge of another soldier.

Later, Praytor would claim in an interview that Miss Hap and he had helped each other: he saved her life, and she made sure he didn't lose his humanity in the midst of war.

Myth: Pregnant women can't live with cats.

Cats can sometimes be infected with a parasite called toxoplasmosis, which can be expelled through their feces.

If a pregnant woman catches this parasite, it can sometimes cause birth defects or miscarriages, and that's something we would want to avoid.

Cleaning the litter box daily will solve this.

It's not advisable to leave the litter box full for more than a day, as that could increase the infection.

If you need to clean the litter box, you should use gloves.

The best thing to do is to have someone else clean the box and thus completely avoid the problem.

78

Myth: Cats don't like babies.

Babies are unpredictable, smell different from people, make different movements than adults, and have stinky diapers.

I think this could be partly true because it's not that they don't like babies, it's just that they are different from the people they are used to.

**Myth: Cats and dogs
don't get along.**

There are many homes where both
dogs and cats are present and
they get along perfectly fine.

Just as there are some people who
don't get along, sometimes a dog
and a cat have the same problem.

I think it depends more on the
personality of the dog and cat
whether they get along.

80

They fall better from great heights.

It's said that cats always land on their feet.

This is possible thanks to their vestibular system, which tells them the position of their head relative to the ground while they fall.

They first turn the upper part of their body and then the lower part, landing on their cushions to cushion the impact.

The greater the falling distance, the more time they have to get in the correct position.

That's why many veterinarians see more serious injuries in parachuting cats that fall from low heights.

This obviously has a limit, as it doesn't mean that a cat can survive a fall from a skyscraper.

The color of a cat's fur can influence their survival.

Tabby or striped cats can better blend in with their natural environment and therefore have a higher chance of going unnoticed by predators and prey.

Additionally, it has been shown that these cats tend to live longer in rural areas.

On the other hand, in urban environments, black or black and white cats tend to be the ones that adapt best.

It is believed that this is because these colors allow them to blend in during the night and in urban areas with little light.

Additionally, there is a popular belief associating black cats with bad luck or witchcraft, which can lead to them being less adopted and, therefore, reproducing more and thriving in urban areas.

It is important to note that a cat's survival depends not only on the color of their fur, but also on other factors such as health, age, and diet, among others.

82

Cats played an important role in the culture of ancient Mesopotamia, including the Sumerian civilization that developed in the region now known as Iraq.

The Sumerians considered cats to be divine beings and worshipped them as symbols of the goddess of fertility and war, Inanna.

Numerous representations of cats have been found in Sumerian art, dating back to the third millennium BC.

In some of these representations, cats appear alongside the goddess Inanna, in others they are shown in hunting poses, and in others, they are simply depicted as domestic animals.

The Sumerians valued cats for their ability to hunt mice and other rodents that could damage crops and stored food.

For this reason, cats remained very popular domestic animals in Sumerian culture and became highly prized objects of trade.

83

Ailurophobia: Fear of cats.

A person with a phobia of cats does not show the same reaction to other types of felines.

That is, they do not have aversion to lynxes, tigers, lions, etc...

They can go to zoos and even show attraction to them.

However, they are unable to enter a room where there is a cat.

84

Ailurophobia: causes and treatment.

<u>Causes:</u>

-Negative past experiences with cats. Having been scratched or bitten by these animals at some point in childhood can trigger a traumatic memory.

-In some cases, fear of an animal can be transmitted from parents to children. It is enough for a parent to show repulsion towards cats for children to end up developing a phobia.

-In a large number of cases, fear of cats can arise without a specific trigger.

<u>Treatment:</u>

-Exposure therapy. In this case, it would involve bringing the person closer to those anxious stimuli (cats), to mediate cognitive and emotional reactions.

-Cognitive-behavioral therapy is the most suitable for enabling the person to handle phobias well. Thanks to it, we can detect maladaptive thoughts, regulate emotions and incorporate more adjusted behaviors.

-Relaxation and breathing techniques are also very suitable in these situations.

85

Can cats be vegan?

There are not enough studies to demonstrate that applying this type of diet has resulted in a greater number of deaths and/or diseases.

On the contrary, there is documented research carried out by the University of Pennsylvania, in which they compared 34 cats fed a homemade or commercial vegetarian diet versus 52 cats fed a conventional diet.

In this study, no notable differences were seen in elements such as blood concentration of cobalamin and taurine.

86

Dreaming about a cat.

It is linked to creativity, as the cat can signify wisdom and our spiritual side.

Due to its stealthy and bold character, the cat also represents intuition, independence, and our wilder side.

Therefore, it should be positive, but it depends on how the cat is, how it makes us feel, how the animal behaves, and how we react.

The cat can also be interpreted as a mysterious being that hides something, which can be dangerous and can attack you suddenly.

This is often interpreted as a warning that someone is trying to deceive or harm us.

The feline is a symbol that can mean different things depending on who dreams it, their beliefs, fears, fantasies, and phobias.

What does it mean to dream that a cat attacks me?

It usually represents your enemies, whether they are people, events, or situations.

Dreaming that a cat attacks you is a symbol of the struggle against what is your enemy.

It is important to note who wins the battle in the dream, whether it's the cat or you.

In reality, a cat can hurt you with an attack by scratching or biting you, but it doesn't have enough strength or size to "win a fight" symbolically speaking.

Therefore, if the cat wins the battle in the dream, it means you are not confronting that fear or enemy with the strength and effort it deserves.

On the contrary, if you manage to remove the cat and chase it away, it means you are overcoming that obstacle that bothers you.

What does it mean to dream of the death of a cat?

If in the dream, you have killed the cat because it was attacking or scratching you, it could be that you are overcoming that fear or obstacle we talked about earlier.

If the cat appears dead, but you have nothing to do with it, or if you hear it being killed but do not intervene, it is usually related to a lack of independence or autonomy.

Maybe you feel suffocated for some reason that is pressing on your subconscious, and that is why it sends you alerts.

This symbolism is also often associated with dreams of cats drowning, because of the feeling of suffocation and anguish.

When both dead and live cats appear in the dream, it can mean an inner conflict in which you will have to decide, and which is crucial in your life.

Sometimes in dreams with a dead cat, blood also appears.

Blood symbolizes life, the essential, so it can mean the fear of losing something really important to you.

89

What does dreaming of a black cat mean?

In many places, black cats are associated with bad luck, so in a way, that message is engraved in our subconscious.

And even though we know that black cats are wonderful, we link the color black with something dark.

Dreaming of black cats is interpreted as fear or doubt of something hidden.

It is often associated with fears, concerns, inner problems that we do not want to face.

It is a way of alerting us about something important that we have inside and that we are not allowing to flourish.

The black cat is symbolizing something hidden, but also that part of power and wisdom that it represents: it is an invitation to reflect on what it is that you are not letting out.

On the other hand, if the feeling we have is that the black cat symbolizes an external danger, it may be representing deceit.

90

What does dreaming of white cats mean?

White is usually interpreted as illusions,
hopes, desires, or goals.

And the way we relate to the white cat will
influence how it makes us feel and therefore
what it symbolizes in our dream.

When the white cat runs away in the dream, it is
interpreted as an obstacle or something we
have to reach to achieve our goal.

The feeling and meaning will be different
if we manage to "catch" the cat or not.

A white, beautiful, and affectionate cat usually
represents something good; but sometimes this
symbol has another interpretation, for example,
if the cat suddenly attacks us or does
things that make us feel bad.

In that case, the kitty symbolizes deceit, as it
shows a beautiful face but is treacherous.

91

What does dreaming of kittens mean?

This dream is usually positive.

It is usually interpreted as a transition towards your independence, and depending on how the kitten is, it will be a simple transition or a strong struggle.

Another quite common meaning is to relate the kitten to something fragile, especially with a person whom we consider that we have to protect.

That is why many times baby kittens are interpreted as children, and hence many pregnant women dream of kittens during the 9 months.

What does a cat seek when sleeping with people?

-Temperature: They usually seek warmth, whether it's in the only sunbeam that enters the house, on radiators, blankets, and even on you. Cats seek warmth when resting, and they usually achieve it by sleeping in your bed, under your duvet, or even on top of you.

-Comfort and security: Cats are always aware of their surroundings, and even though they may appear to be sound asleep, they are alert to any loud or strange noises. Sleeping close to you provides them with a sense of security and mental tranquility.

-Relationship with you: The closeness of the relationship between the cat and you varies depending on the cat and you. However, it's common for the feline to miss you (especially if you've been away from home for hours) and want to take advantage of the night by being close to you. In litters, cats often huddle together to give each other warmth, comfort, and protection. Cats see you as one of their own, so headbutting, cuddling, and sleeping together are part of being "just another cat" to them.

93

Why do cats change hair color?

-Due to genetics. Some breeds are genetically programmed to change color according to the ambient temperature, such as Siamese cats.

-Due to age. Another common factor is that changes occur with age, typically in two periods: when the cat stops being a kitten (many cats experience changes in their coat until they are 5-6 months old) and when the cat is very old (in some cases, gray hair may appear, which is not a health problem).

-Due to sunlight. A cat that is exposed to a lot of sunlight may end up with a hair color that is lighter than its original color. In black cats, this often results in a reddish or brownish coat.

-Due to diet. Changes in hair color may indicate a lack of some vital nutrient or element. A veterinarian will determine the diagnosis.

-Due to health problems. In these cases, the change is usually more abrupt. Some of the most common reasons are stress, problems with the hair growth cycle, vitiligo and alopecia, and an imbalance of essential elements such as a lack of tyrosine or copper, as well as an excess of zinc.

94

Extinct breed: Aztec cat.

They were hairless for most of the year, except in winter when a light layer of hair grew on their tail and back, likely to protect them from the cold.

They were light grey with flesh-colored tints and had very long eyebrows and whiskers.

According to records, they were 25% smaller than short-haired cats.

They enjoyed taking hot baths, sleeping under the sheets, cuddling, and were playful and careful climbers on people.

They also got along well with the house dog.

Extinct breed: Eskimo cat.

This is one of those supposed extinct cat breeds that is so rare it is considered an urban legend today.

The history of the Eskimo cat dates back to the 19th century.

The idea is that these cats developed in Pittsburgh (USA) due to the need to eradicate rat pests in refrigeration plants.

The legend says that so many generations were raised in the environment of a "big fridge" that the cats developed a very dense fur, thick tails, and their ears had become similar to those of lynxes.

They also felt more comfortable in darkness and cold than in full daylight and warmer climates.

An article about this new cat breed was even written in the New York Times in 1894, and soon the story spread like wildfire, also appearing in other newspapers.

Cats' penises have spikes.

It is one of the strangest parts of their anatomy, and the main reason is that the glans is covered with up to 200 keratin spikes called spines.

These spines are oriented backward, so penetration itself is not painful for the female, but the withdrawal of the penis is commonly considered painful, although not entirely clear.

During mating, the spines serve several functions: they clean the semen duct of previous males, which is useful given that females mate frequently during estrus, stimulate the male for a faster ejaculation, and keep the female "hooked" until the end.

Additionally, the scraping of the vaginal walls stimulates the female's ovulation, with more effectiveness the more times mating is repeated.

4 changes that occur in the behavior of a pregnant cat:

-More hours of sleep than usual, as the body needs all the energy it can gather for the development of the fetuses. In addition, the hormonal changes of pregnancy also cause drowsiness.

-Less appetite, which will then increase. During the first few weeks, your cat may eat less than usual, mainly due to nausea and discomfort. When these symptoms decrease, her food intake will gradually increase until doubling her usual ration in the final phase of pregnancy.

-She may be very affectionate or more distant: some cats are more affectionate and demand a lot of attention during pregnancy, while others become aloof and solitary. If your cat is pregnant, her attitude will vary in one of these two directions.

-Nesting: as the delivery approaches, your cat will start working to create a small nest. She may move her bed to a more secluded corner and may bring cat toys, towels, dolls... it is a natural behavior that you should not interfere with.

98

The pregnancy of cats lasts on average 9 weeks, but can range from 58 to 67 days.

During this period, the pregnant cat will experience physical and behavioral changes.

The most noticeable physical changes during a cat's pregnancy include an increase in the size of the abdomen, nipples becoming larger and pinker, and there may be a decrease in appetite in the first few weeks of gestation.

It is also possible for the pregnant cat to become more affectionate or protective of her territory.

It is important that the pregnant cat receives adequate and sufficient nutrition during the gestation period, as this will influence the health of the kittens.

In addition, it is recommended to take the cat for regular veterinary check-ups to ensure that everything is going well during the pregnancy.

99

How many kittens can a cat have?

The number can vary greatly, but it's common for a cat to give birth to between 3 and 6 kittens.

Typically, a first-time mother cat will have fewer offspring than an experienced one: she'll have an average of 3 or 4 kittens in her first litter and 5 or 6 in subsequent litters.

During her lifetime, a wild cat can have up to 100 offspring.

It's important to note that the number of kittens a cat can have depends on several factors, such as breed, age, health, and nutrition.

For example, Persian and Siamese breeds tend to have smaller litters, while mixed-breed or stray cats tend to have larger litters.

100

How can you tell if a cat is going to give birth soon?

The signs that may indicate that your cat is about to give birth are the following:

-She constantly licks her vulva.

-She may have a bloody discharge from the vulva, although you may not see it if the cat licks it away.

-If you look closely, you may notice gentle contractions in the cat's swollen belly.

-The cat is very restless, pacing back and forth and meowing a lot.

-The nesting process speeds up, or if the nest is already prepared, the cat retreats to it frequently.

101

How long does it take for a cat to go into heat after giving birth?

After giving birth, the cat's body goes through a period of recovery and healing.

Typically, during the first few weeks after giving birth, the cat is not in heat and is not fertile.

However, as she recovers and her hormone levels normalize, she may go into heat again within a period of 4 to 8 weeks.

It's important to note that even though the cat may go into heat again after this period of time, it's recommended to wait at least 6 months before allowing her to become pregnant again.

This will ensure that she has enough time to fully recover from the previous birth and avoid health problems related to too frequent pregnancies.

Additionally, cat overpopulation is a serious problem in many areas, so it's important to carefully control cat reproduction.

If you have enjoyed our book of cat curiosities, we would love for you to share your experience on Amazon and give us your opinion about the book.

We understand that these types of curiosities can be very interesting and useful for those who want to learn more about their pets, and your review can help others discover all the wonders of the feline world.

We know that writing a review can seem a bit overwhelming, but your opinion is very valuable to us.

It helps us improve and create more useful content for our readers, and of course, it motivates us to keep working hard to provide the best possible content.

We appreciate your support and hope that you have enjoyed reading our book as much as we enjoyed writing it.

Thank you for sharing your experience with us!

Printed in Great Britain
by Amazon

24868317R00062